KNOWLEDGE

For David Burnett,
    with best wishes.

Michael Heller

Knowledge

Michael Heller

SUN

NEW YORK 1979

ACKNOWLEDGEMENTS

"Bialystok Stanzas" appeared in *American Poetry Review*, "Objurgations" in *Boundary 2*, "And if the Truth Were" in *Chelsea*, "Malaga: The Palace Garden" in *The Cincinnati Review*, "Stele," "Dressed Stone," "Interminglings," "After Montale," "Mourning by the Sea" in *Montemora*, "Postulates," "Knowledge," "The Toast," "Question or Answer Before Threnody," "The Mind's Return," "Poem of America Written on the Five Hundredth Anniversary of Michelangelo's Birth" in *Occurrence*, "In the Park," "On the Beach," *"Speculum Mortis,"* "Seeing the Pain Again" in *Pequod*, "Florida Letter," "Near Guernsey" in *Pulp*, "At Albert's Landing" in *Origin*, "Manhattan Spleen" in *The Atlantic Review*, "Stanzas on Mount Elbert" and "Visitor at Acabonac" in *Confrontation*.

"Postulates" was the recipient of a Poetry in Public Places Award and appeared on New York City buses in 1976.

The Poems "At Albert's Landing" and "Figures of Speaking" are part of a limited edition entitled *Figures of Speaking* published by Walter Hamady at the Perishable Press in 1977.

The author wishes to thank the New York State Council on the Arts for the Creative Artists Public Service Fellowship in Poetry which was of assistance in completing this book of poems.

Printed in the United States of America

First Edition

Library of Congress Cataloging in Publication Data

Heller, Michael, 1937-
    Knowledge.

    I. Title.
PS3558.E4762K58   811'.5'4   79-25843
ISBN 0-915342-30-8

The publication of this book is supported by grants from the National Endowment for the Arts in Washington, D.C., a Federal agency, and the New York State Council on the Arts.

To JA

Contents

I

Visitor at Acabonac

Last night's rain
Washed mud into the estuaries;
Today the water is burnished, impermeable,

Non-reflective under the sun's flat hit.
Down the beach, some distance from the bathers,
Gulls walk along a sandy ledge.

The moon afloat in daylight,
A chalky hallucinatory eye
Above the tide's grey dead sluggish weight,

Suggesting only
What is isolate, what cannot link. This is
A world of forms, of manners

Of voices and cries of birds
Shredded in the reeds,
In the stunted pines:

These intact islands
Amid these minor eddies of the human
With their small distances to be spanned.

At the harbor mouth,
One comes upon shingled houses
Desolate on hummocks, on low spits of sand,

And the white sails of pleasure boats
Catch sun like perfect messages,
Perfect dreams that ply between.

3

The Toast

Dapples this glass, the wine—
The hearth coals
Embered flies in its fine crystal

You across the room—elbow
Or strand of hair, pinioned
In the reflection
Amid red liquid, amid red glowings:
Difficult loveliness—unknowable star
Of this warm composition

Let the eye go
From there to you? Let it
Break from the glass
Where lingering spares the shock
Of the next mote of deadly beauty

And now, there's but a word,
Another pledge of the voice
Which bears despair in its tremolo
As we both swear to the image unproved
Meant to shatter
This refracted prison

Knowledge

To think a man might dream against this
This something simpler than metaphor

The world
Which spoke back
In facts, to him

That heavy pageantry

Yet when the life or when the bed
Was empty
He'd lay his head
Among the voices of the dead

It was his child and his childhood
It was coats and books
Heaped in a room
Toys and an ache

Leaving Grand Central

for George Oppen

On the way to a sunlight of lawns
And suburbs, to find oneself caught
In the train's swaying,

The smudged windows' thistling
Of a few lights. At the windows,
With faces set,

To look out past
Dusty reflections, past
Girders crossed and blackened with smoke

Which hold the roof, the careless
Heaven of the paving above one's head. This
Is not our world, one wants to say,

This channel which will spew us
Into a daylight of blocks and blocks
Of utter ravishment.

And as the bridge is crossed
In the windless day
Barely a current moves

Under the imaged buildings.
And what little guilty cry the heart makes
For safety in escape—

To be borne past
The towers and low rows of flats,
To see behind the brick and glass

Those trapped in the real apparition—
Here the window does not mirror back.

Florida Letter

They come here
To repeal a northern drabness

To find frivolity
A recompense of straw hats
Of colorful clothes

They want the sunlight
Which dispels the chill

But the hard glare withers
The eye slits on death

Watching the wave's glitter
As it eats away the shore

Only time itself is the obdurate
Against which the heart leaps

And the white hotels
Are like bone against the sky

This was no one's future
No one's dream

Only the poor power
To make a dream imaginable

Question or Answer before Threnody

for my father

I. Already, the hibiscus blossoms

    Its odor on the late August air
    Mingling with late season parchness of grass and palm

    By the canal's edge
    The reds and browns
    Are given back their mirrored figures
    In the almost still deep green

    Already, the lizard skirts
    From bush to bush

    Its eye in its round horn
    Alert to light and shade

    And do you see the blank sky's whiteness
    Mirroring nothingness

    Or the pale blench from color
    At the red hibiscus's center

II. Small triumphs surround you
    The photos on the wall
    The plaques and gavel

    The darkened brass
    Inscribed with names

    Trophies which halt nothing

    Your goodwill
    And virtue are not mine
    To judge. Rather, I see

    Your face pinched,
    Tears at your eyes

    Perhaps you foresee
    What cannot last:

    This youth, *this* strength
    To gaze upon
    Your sons and daughter

    These shred-ends

    Disentangling bonds
    Of the human

III. Story of our lives
Like the story of our differences

Like beach glass
The sea throws up among the shells

The filmy winks of purpose

Father upon father—
The chance-haunted voices—

Together for a time
We live out this resort life
Of beaches

Together
We found it foreign to us both

Even today, looking
At the wall of palms

The road's turn
And the bay holding
A more vivid moon than I remember

Who can say
This world?

I know of youth
Spent and respent

And the eye follows
The efflorescent track

To the sky's white stone
The stars melt in its light

Never has it shone so much as now
For neither love nor indifference

Miami—NYC
Aug.—Sept., 1975

11

II

Bialystok Stanzas

(from a book of old pictures)

1

Light—
The scene filled with photographer's light

This sparsely furnished room
In the corner of which
A china-closet Ark

The old men
Under green shaded bulbs
Reading *Torah*

The prayers are simple,
To what they think larger
Than themselves
—the place almost bare,
Utterly plain

The flat white light
Adds no increment
But attention

He sits in the armchair
Beside his bed

In his hands
A Yiddish paper

On his head
A high black
Pointed *yarmulka*

The room's things
Furnished by donation
Reads a small brass plaque
Above the headboard of the bed

A bed, a hat upon his head

A *yiskor* glass, the candle for the dead
Burnt down, the wax scraped out

He uses it for drinking

Shiny linoleum
You can almost
Smell the pine oil

The beds
A few feet apart

So the old men
Tired of the world
In the evening
Can face each other
And talk

But now the shades are half pulled up
Sun streams in the windows

The room almost empty
But for the two directors
Sitting stiffly on chairs
Who, like the white painted beds,
Seem supremely
Official

At one side
Two grey bedridden men
Finished too with dignity
Are giggling

The old bind with phylacteries
—between the leather turns
The pinched flesh bulges, the old
Skin, the hairs burn

As if to do this is also
For the pain
—to explain
To Him of what it is
They are made

Thus, why they fail

This one and that one
Look like madmen
With their long wisps of hair

They scream: I chant, I dance
Like a crab

In the room the women wail
A plangent erotic note
Their loins itch with double fire
As he in topcoat-who-is-blessed
Bestirs them
Screams their demons back

Until their innocence
Stands naked as desire

Oy, Oy
He whirls, he spins
Till the beard is out
From his face like a flag

And in wild wisdom
Throws her to the boards

She, who would
That next instant
Have pulled him down to her
But for the trick
Of the ritual

THE JEWISH FIRE COMPANY

There was one fireman none knew
Neither his family nor friends
He had good eyes, though they looked
A little wild. He was sent
To the watchtower

One day, almost at once,
Two fires broke out in town
The hasid grocer's
And a gentile butcher

The fireman warned
Of the butcher's blaze
But said nothing about the grocer
Whose place burned to the ground

When what he had failed to do
Was discovered and explanation demanded
He said: those who do not
Follow our God's way
Must be helped
And those who do
Must accept his justice

— — — — — — — — — — — — — — — — — —

This one joined
So the young ladies
Should see him in uniform

They did
And flattered the brass and the leather
But not him

Finally, he charmed a farm girl
Of pious family into the fields

And in the manner of the orthodox
Threw his cap to the hay
Where he thought to take her

To his delight, she bent toward
The straw, raising her skirt
As she kneeled. Suddenly,
She whisked the cap up
Tucked it in her girdle and ran away

So ashamed was he
The next day he left for Warsaw

Years later, the farm girl
Placed the cap on her first-born's head

TERRIBLE PICTURES

Page 147

Snow—
A group of people
Awkwardly caught

They have just discovered
The photographer, and he, them

The old man with the sack
Who has turned
Shrugs his disbelief into the lens

No sense of emergency
In the pose
Could be as real

Page 153

Grimly
They lie closely packed
Upon each other
In the mass grave

Looking now
Like figures of saints
Carved across cathedral doors

—but beyond image or irony,
The empty wrongness.

Here, all death
Was made untimely

Page 163, Caption:

"fought in the streets to the very end
and perished by his own hand
with the last remaining bullet"

Page 164, Caption:

"died in the ghetto"

Page 166, Caption:

"fell in battle...1944"

Page 168, Caption:

"killed..."

Page 157, Burnt Synagogue

This light—
A river through which
Another life poured

Figure and ground
Of how the dark
Informs the light

Brings forth bodies, faces
Brings forth
The things of the earth
That we see to completion
—beloved, hated—

But that life was broken forever
Here, look, look, this is but
Its mirror

Only the mirror remains

And gone—
Whole peoples are gone
To horror beyond remonstrance—

Freitogdige
Donershtogdige
Shabbosdige
Consumed in those fires

Words can add nothing
That flame itself was without a light

The Yiddish names above were those given by the citizens of Bialystok to the victims of three mass executions: "the Friday dead," "the Thursday dead," "the Saturday dead."

FROM THE ZOHAR

The blue light
      having devoured
All beneath it:
      the priests,
The Levites, etc....
      Now the prayerful ones
Gather
      at the flames' base
Singing and meditating
      while above the lamp glows,
The lights, in unity, are merged
Illumined world
      in which above and below
Are blessed

SENILE JEW

One God. One boiled egg.
Thirty *dy-yanus*, and the Paradise
Not yet given a number.

Eight nights, eight lights
Which break the dark
Like a cat's wink.

I think the boot is not gone—
Whose boot? I ask
Do you wear the boot?
Or does he who wears the boot
Wear you?

Coat of my pain, cloth
Of pain, winding sheet of
My horror. Just a rag,
Just a *shmata*. You
Are not my pain, not you.
My pain is me: I am the Jew.

III

After Montale

Nothing which seems particularly large.
The poet catches the mere termite
Busy at its burrowing. Then that fellow
Disappears, and only the hole
Is left.

All this took was time.
And we wonder what it is
That time itself creates or excretes
Or simply disappears into. What hole
It leaves.

Dressed Stone

In the image sought
As something so primitive
Something it must have said
To those who looked
And from that articulation
Things had to be named
And the mystery held in love
By that name...

So, in winter
The slabs lie jumbled in the snow
Half-exposed beside the building site
Their aspect fierce,
Close to the monolith
They've been cut from

Until employed in the design
And thin tar strips
Placed between saw-marked surfaces
Where as night falls
A slight shift of temperature
Will take a meaning

Then the eye, by habit, strays
To the moon
Riding the unsheathed girders

And how beside use, how
Close love must be
To the cold light
Touching stone
Across the distance

The Mind's Return

to D.

Do you remember
By this small river, the Seine,
We had come

The sun was setting

In the light which held
The building stones glowed red
The heat was on the air
The air one breath respiring

This true, unalterable…

In that place
Our bodies partook
Of that dreamlike dance
—the strict simple principles
Of density and mass—
Substance of the mind

In that city, where histories and their dying
Are equally grand, equally absurd
Those engendered phantoms
Pressed from the heart
To inform the real—all we will know?

How we bore those marks
The living and the living rubble

Yet nothing at last seems ours
Different, that is, from being mine or yours alone

And the mind seeks
Among those signs
Rising to the rigor of the world

Where the glass of buildings flared
In the sun's fire—
A sheet of flame—

And the stone
Was for a moment after the sun set
Still warm to the touch

Malaga: The Palace Garden

I think we have lost
The theme which is recovery

But the source
Is followed out

The trace of branched duct
To flowerbed and pool

To seek the thing
Which forced this shape
Which feeds so much
And determines so much

To find it inconsequential
—some pebble
At the gate of a sluice

There, the water whirls
And discord lashes in the channel,
In the beveled stone

And what is lovely plays against,
Against even the discord
And the discord imparts to it
The hidden harmony
Thought better

Yet, this is still
Not the wonder
Which annuls
The iron ring in the wall
Or the shine on the Guardia's leather

And here the stone rests on stone
And we want to note that this thing matters:
How the builder's art has made this place

So the sea wind blows back
And mixes salt with the tree's fragrance
Along the flagged walk which runs the rim
Above the city

Down there, the bull dies, I suppose,
That the bull-god may live on

Yet we have found it hard
To picture dungeons pitched in stone,

To imagine for the unbeliever
The gilded Allahs of that page
Were heavier than the sun...

The music of the caged birds,
Of the water's purl
Is both sad and joyful

As is the burnished handiwork
Of the chambers of the King
Before whose doors, power withers love

Above is the frieze, the running lattice
Of the grille,

The trapped energy of image

Fearful nuance—by this
Are we lulled from terrors and greeds—

These acts
Which would supplant their beginnings
With their consequence—

Yet in time one is trapped
Between the beauty and the fault

Evil is victorious
The wheel does not stop

The quarry's stone
Shows even in the chisel work
The unmeant markings

Poem of America Written on
the Five Hundredth Anniversary
of Michelangelo's Birth

Freedom, after all? The train
Moving through *the land of the free*

From the embankment: the highway,
The tract, the house: destiny's

Manifest. The senator on the podium's
from sea to shining sea, which now

From any small vantage, such sense
Of sadness. A few trees

In the straight ruled streets, barely
The hint of contour, as though

The world were at last possessed.
Movement and stasis. The buildings

And shapes under the open air.
And the dust from the railbed

Glints in passage, like the slave's
Form, half-carved, escaping from the rock,

Edges aglow in the museum light. Finished.
Finished. Dust

Dancing in the air in the knowledge
Of limit's time and limit's place

Tormenting dance of emergence.

And If the Truth Were

and if the truth were
that Icarus sought
the sun

wouldn't it also be true
that his father
passed on that love
to the boy
as fathers will
—dooming them both

so that Icarus died
perhaps as the old man
would have wanted to

while Daedalus went on
like a youth
with the bitter mockery
of invention

In the Park

On the bench,
Sitting in the woman's lap, a grown man

A *pieta* seen
At ten removes of time and place

Making the story's end
Suddenly its beginning

Mother, I remember
That red peaked broken union
Which was your breast

And know no older wound
Of memory

Invited and lost,
Invited and fled

And my life again a broken tale
—not for truth, but *to please you*—
Which I have to tell

At Albert's Landing

(with my son)

I. The path winds. You are around a bend
   Unseen. But your voice
   Crackles in the walkie-talkie
   You made me bring. "Here's a leaf,
   A tree." The detail,
   Not the design, excites you.
   I don't know what to say.
   After months in the city,
   I'm feeling strange in the woods.

II. Spongy ground.
    Matted leaves
    Beneath which lie
    Dirt, bones, shells.
    Late April: milky light
    And warmth. Thinnest odors rise.
    In the middle of one's life
    More things connect
    With dying, what's come,
    What's over.

III. It is said
     That what exists is like the sky
     Through which clouds pass. I suspect
     That mine is a poetry of clouds.
     Above me, some wispy tuft catches sun
     In an interesting way. *The naked very thing.*
     I'm glad of this, don't look
     In the billowy mass
     For the teased-out shape
     Of a horse's head or a bird's wing.
     Yet finding it now and then,
     Unsummoned: some thought or image,
     Recalling how each
     Depends on each.

IV. Together we follow the trail's twists
    Until the pond.
    There, two white egrets
    Stand against the high brown grass.
    Intent watching
    Is almost timeless, but some noise
    One of us makes scares them off.
    They rise over our heads, circle
    Out of sight. Strange sadness
    Grips me. The after-image
    Of their shapes still burns.

V. Here we are in some fugal world.
    Tree branches make a kind of tent.
    And the squirrel, when he eats,
    Looks like a little man. And here
    You fling your arms out
    Whirling around at the frightened
    Skimming ducks. The duck's eye,
    Like ours, must be its center. We
    Are alone, rooted in our aloneness.
    And yet things lean and lean,
    Explaining each other and not themselves.
    I call you; it's time to go.

VI. Different as the woods are
    This is no paradise to enter or to leave.
    Just the real, and a wild nesting
    Of hope in the real
    Which does not know of hope.
    Things lean and lean, and sometimes
    Words find common centers in us
    Resonating and filling speech.
    Let me know a little of you.

IV

Objurgations

1

Talk in the room
The voices thick with lyric

And to hear the facts bend in
Deflected from the absolutes
Of wall and floor
Of limit and definition

To speak of things
In terror
In the brutal cognates
Of love and desire

Until, like the floor's worn boards
Beneath which gape the hollows of the building
One's meaning gains some small shine

Rooms scar the mind. Empty rooms
Which punish for love. Yet the place
Is fulfilled, indicative...

Shut the door, draw the blinds—
No closure here
But that of carpentry

The walls, the bric-a-brac are heralds
And extend themselves

It could as well happen beyond these walls
As well in the world, the part-willed
Of the world...

There, to have arrived severally
Perhaps interested
To consider exchange

To equilibrate the goods and lives

To watch the crowds move, reflect
Make over their movement into purpose

To walk, to be buried,
To be huddled in their bulk

To go from them cheated and hated
And to hear later, others felt that way...

Yet, in the numberless storms of event
To find no one
Who meant that this should happen

To watch them moving
And the moving
Either lovely or ugly

To discover cause
And no place closed to it

To read from the streetsigns, placards,
Shops, the days of traffic and trafficking
Seemingly impossible of error

Thus, to fear a mystery less than certainty
To fear the terror of explanation

To impose rules, to judge,
To discover motive and reason
To go beyond reason

Until, like the monkey in the photo
One is stranded on *The Structure of the World*
Grinning from that bare pole

Which is
The danger of the literal

Meaning:
To search for what you might love
—not what might love you—

To find up close
It is still what it is

To know the gods have fled
To know myth only as this moment

To know the breast
Which bears your head and your humility
Is not your mother's breast

This is the danger
Of the literal

Where is that moment
When the poem like a worm
Painfully parts the tissue

Spiraling down the psyche
Dark turn on turn
Toward some light of true cause

Finding, nibbling, feeding on that cause
Till it's we who are the worm
In the poem, and cringe in its light

For this is how the world
We call beautiful
Came into being

And the worlds through which
We move, even its trees and rocks
Are the absurd works of men

Things to which
They have given beauty
Only half theirs to give

And it is conquered
Even with ecology, finished
And only that not begun
Not by us at least, has any power

Thus, whether the word is found
Or finds us, it is inserted in history
Though now we are told
Is no time for a *bon mot*

To suspect and not from error
That one seeks an identity
Of a mathematical sort

Standing in the world,
Functioning as some imperfect
Equal sign

Because both sides of these equations
Always balance—there is
No other way to look at it

Therefore, the horror must be let in
And like Tu Fu, one keeps
Music and rites to conquer his failings

To keep a machine clean
In a filthy time, to seek
Meaning for compassion,
Meaning: don't let self-definition
Perish

To be condemned thus
From the beginning—no time
When it was different and not different

No time when
All this seemed more expendable

Like the newly hatched duck,
Placed beside the basketball
—took it for its mother—

That we're determined or not
Is beside the point

If we're born
With attraction towards a thing
Even the wrong thing
It's also towards ourselves

Neither the mob at the spectacle
Nor Homer at the wars
Is a singular

If I must prove this
And not do so by exception
—that I, for the sake of hatred

Might have lusted for a woman
Then grew to love her deeply
For having let me come

Isn't it to say, the poem
Is now and then our master
It bears our beatitude for what's most unholy
Even our outsized hate

So *thralldom!*
And the whole schema
You little shits

Which I would bomb and bulldoze
If I were King

Ha!

The cities and the bluntly shining stars
Clusters that can gleam with use

A dispensary: *grab for them*
The thing we're taught

As indeed, the last word
Of the poet's reading was "stars"

And after, we walked to the pier
One star in the sky

I said it was Venus, imagined
It the star

Which gathers love and world

And in the half-truth of the metaphor
The point it holds is clear and steady

And yet the small lights in streets
The strung necklace of the bridge

No more than complement

Light among buildings
Catching the sharp edge of stone

Familiar yet isolate:
He, this brick, this city

Stories in the streets
Places given names

Memory and fantasy made real...

To feel one had the meaning wrong
The error not of increment but tone
—not of the Gods, not even of their house

But we had seen the thing like a god
Or like some manufactured part
Sitting in the sun

Yet to tell of the difference
Between our worship of the dream
And the worship done in dreams

To wake in that room, that world,
The sky grown light

The spectacle of building tops and streets
Plunged in monstrous otherness

To know meaning and remembrance
Dwell no place
But in the blood

V

Postulates

Loss is more complex than gain
Though neither completely understood.
One remembers
He was five, six, seven years old.
To the fact of the memory
The memory stands
As an axe to wood. Wood, ourselves,
In the streamings and contours,
The roughened grain.

Make a mark on me.

Speculum Mortis

Angled toward you in the glass,
Mind wanting ease
I think, Mother, we scarcely look alike.

And yet, the 'doctor of grief'
May do no more than be a little slothful.

And the light is
As from a non-reflective dark

And invades the mirror's space,
A hollow strangely lit,

A light, sourceless,
Radiant

As any truth,
Disfiguring all one thinks one is.

Stele

for Jane

Otherwise goes past all object
The light blazes on the stone

The light which also falls
On you
          And I touch you
Almost as I touch death
Following where the light goes
My voice half-raised in respite

And I know then
What is beyond an earthly love,
What escapes the chisel's work:
The hurting godhead within the stone
—all that we wish
Might want us—sealed away

And when thought and sight
Are taken ·to the marble's grain
—held there by cupidity of beauty

That death I know
Is but a light on form

Interminglings

to J.A.

I. Sun on the begrimed windows.
Light and dust curiously arrayed,

Infused with each other, falling
On the bed, on ourselves where we lie.

Finite life in the pattern's
Verge and shift, in the hovering dust.

In the beam's slant,
Designs almost infinite.

I know, in my heart,
This nature is all aesthetic.
Each, resolved, being something like a story.

Story of ourselves
In these curves and tangles,

In the half-light.
What I wanted to say

Was that in truth, we each
Could have picked, could have
Found ourselves

Among any of these.

II. Many years given
In belief of the body's sadness

A thickness, as of the throat,
In the world.

From there, the voice telling
Into its knotted web
Of glints and darknesses.

Perhaps you are moved as I am,
Lifted in some strange way
By the plunge into sorrows.

Facing each other, these recognitions:
Two small animals, quiverers,

Aware they can be hurt.
And sometimes, nothing,

Not even the severe lines
Of your body, which wildly delight

Bring me this close to you.
For all that is different,

How each in our life
Is alike.

III. We agreed. No one's quite written out
   A philosophy of affluence, least of all
   This affluence I'm feeling today.

   What strikes in the world,
   A curious kind of comfort

   Where bug and leaf, or better, bug
   And garbage in the street, are joined.

   The broken hydrant almost sings a warble.
   The undersides of clouds, sulphurous green and red.

   Crossing the Bowery to your place,
   "marks of weakness, marks of woe".

   Strange, ugliness and loveliness
   Both slash the heart.

   No shelter: we are exposed
   Like the weed shooting through the rubble,

   Like the tree's small roots
   Which curl at the stone, at the broken pipework.

   Almost part of, and not against.

   To imagine this
   Is what is workable.

   That the spring did not come
   To enrage the tree...

   And I think now of the open bow of your back,
   Tremor which ends, which does not end.

   The gesture sears.
   The cursive graves its line in me.

This remains the one gift.
This alone is unconfused.

IV. *Above Westcliffe*

All this living, dying.
The town lights seem barely pinched
Out of the folds of darkness

And the moon, so lovely, so far,
Fullblown tonight into a dream's indifference
Riding solitary above the black pines

The skunk waddles and the deer
Comes to lick at the salt block
Ghastly in the whiteness, perversely
Monumental—

They move with the rest
Through the eye's frame of
This beautiful pointlessness

I too arrive without exactly having
Taken myself—my *self*, whatever,
In this moment, that is.

Where, that depth?

And the chart and the starbook
Are strange counsel. The fixities themselves
Are caught in their slow turn
And go under the world
Like human time, like human death

The candle sputters, dies in the room
Burning all, chair, bed, bodies into shadow
—breast, thigh, you, me
And the light and dark pour their grainy liquid
Into that wave that bears up love, succor, pity
In a transmigratory arc

On the Beach

I. My doctor tells me:
   With your skin, sunlight is dangerous.

   Western Man, I'm hurt, but go armed.
   A broadbrimmed hat, umbrella,
   Lotions which I am told stop light
   But draw flies.

   Sitting there, I read that Montale saw,
   A la Fellini, a monstrous woman
   Plump herself down onto crumbling sand
   And speak Truth.

   I try to spot truth from shade,
   Watching square yards of such flesh
   Baste itself with oil.

   Thou shalt be anointed
   For glamour, youth, illusion,
   The thing to do.

   What I see is that the sun is bright
   And that perhaps suntans, while looking
   Healthy, are deceiving.

   Even here, amid these minor increments
   Of peril, one is consoled. In this
   Careless resort life of beaches
   Deceptions themselves are a kind of truth.

II. The philosopher tells us
   Mentally we are joined to what we look at,
   That seeing can haunt.

   If the wave is rough
   One sits it out, bathing
   In the shade or sun.
   It's as free as this other thing
   The mottled clacking teeth of empty shells
   Can hint at.

   By the path's edge,
   The infectious tick
   Sits on the tip end of the dune grass

   Like one's gaze,
   Ready to be fed
   Ready to install other infusions.

   Above, seabirds wheel —
   Not so much cruelness, but what is actual
   In eye and beak.

   Overhearing that line of Rilke's
   "You must change your life."
   I looked again at the sea's glint.

III. Depending on the weather,
      Yesterday's sandbar
      Is today's dangerous shoal.

      Yesterday's clam,
      Today's 700 beats of a gull's wing.

      The high rump of shingle
      Where the sun fell, in the instant
      When it fell for everyone,
      Is also gone,
      Dredged this winter to make
      A boatman's channel.

      It's not all mechanics, all improvement
      Or all evolution.

      Depending on the weather,
      We play a funny game
      On the beach.

      My son follows me, stamping his feet
      Deliberately into my tracks.

      He says, I don't want to step on a sharp shell
                                        or jellyfish.
      Laughs, Look, Dad, I'm crushing your footprints.

VI

Stanzas on Mount Elbert

Where we climbed in the berserk air
Of trails, sharp spiky views
And dizzying vertigo. I watched
Marmot and pika dart
Among lichen covered rocks
Envying not their agility
But that they survive
On such apparent bleakness.

Then, seeing you on the path above,
Aspen crook in hand, orange poncho
Bannered to the wind, the painter's
Famous *Wanderer in the Clouds*,
Whatever passes between us,
Whoever you are, in that moment
You were a guide to me. We took
The path six inches at a time: with each
Breath a step; with each step a breath,
Sounds of ourselves reverberating
In hollows, in great brown cratered cups of rock
Until what was human seemed to be passing
Into its sheer facticity.

And by the summit, head abuzz in thin air,
Pain or joy or confusion heaped as one
Into the round bulge
Of the mountain's endlessness, it was
Almost too comical to have walked there,
To worship at that feast of obstacles.

And the lakes four thousand feet below
Leered crazily. I think
We were looking back
At what does or does not exist,

What the mind mirrors; something
To which we do not so much return
As turn to, though the turning hurts.

Figures of Speaking

1. From Norman Malcolm's memoir:
   "Wittgenstein liked to draw an analogy
   between philosophical thinking and swimming:
   just as one's body has a natural tendency
   towards the surface and one has to make
   an *exertion* to get to the bottom—so it is
   with thinking."

   Sadness, love, intent. These too are heavy.
   The poet also not a fish
   But an aquanaut in a dangerous medium.

2. In a book on the ancient world
   Reading how grave robbers don't dig
   But drive a bronze rod
   Into the ground
   Until something they hit
   Makes the right sound.

   I think
   I rob my own grave
   When I look at you
   Writing a word,
   Losing myself.

   The marvel in the unexpectedness,
   Not so much sound as recognition—
   As when I found you in a mural
   In that same book,
   A wraith
   Who 4000 years ago
   Danced beside the Indus.

3. The beauty of the older poet's voice
   Punishes me.

What is beautiful must
Or one doesn't believe it.

4. The *whoosh-whoosh* of the inhalator in the hospital room
Counseling patience.

5. Hearing her sing to herself
I knew it was not an aria of the sexual,
Notes of which we would both mount...

Rather, it was the quiet hum
Of the quotidian
Self-involved

By that, saying
I am me, who are you?

6. My little boy.

When I hear him trying out
Words he's learned

Impatient to reach
The matter,

I'm reminded of my own going in...

Not all words sing.

Thinking of poems,
It comes home to me
—the world already existing
Without a name.

Mourning by the Sea

"sough incessant"

Your father died, mine dies.
Mothers, sisters, brothers still.
Dark harbor water mottled green and blue.

Before us on the sand,
The crab claw severed,
The bivalve crushed, the shell in shards.

The *on* then *off* of this is hard.
The place,
The boundary edge—

Where picked from off its ledge
The polyp dissolves
At the gull's stomach wall.

This is not spring; this is not fall.
The brush tips all.
Your eyes, your laugh—

To see one living is to see by half.
The body changes before the eyes:
Dust dark in light the sun burns.

Such light on wavès is curve and turn,
End seeding end.
And the image then that wants to come,

Thin as air,
Is nothing but words: terror and fear,
No self and no recurrence.

Near Guernsey

In the guide book:
The account of a Mormon woman

Trading her wedding ring
For a sack of flour

To know
What's not in the story

How life exhausts
Each symbol, each ideology,
Leaving only itself

Not that something thought sacred
Was traded for bread

But that the bread thereby
Becomes the sacrament

Seeing the Pain Again

'Personal' histories.
Like seeing black bushes
Against the night

Or the moon's ghostly
Paring of itself
Swirling in clouds

Almost the reversal
Of identities, roles...

Nothing to turn from,
Not even the pain I can't answer for

Here in the mountains,
In the clear air,
One faces the whole thing—
Yours, mine—

An ocean's worth,
Suspended
Amid the great waves of rigid stone.
Something in which the whole can barely move:
Shocks, faults, tides of shale...

Thinking of how each is hurt,
Even if it is past, even
If it is no longer seen or touched,

Contact remains.
It ravages in the confusion between us
Like a storm at a distance

Undecipherable, private
But for the lightning's flash
Which lets one see nothing but itself

Releasing into something true:
One dark outlined against a dark.

Manhattan Spleen

The trees: knobbed fingers grasping at the greyish mottled sky. We had come from downtown to see a friend who was appearing in a ballet, and, since there was time before the performance, we, like others around us, sat on the benches before the massively constructed concerthalls, pale stone edifices which seemed designed to defend the arts rather than house them.

As we sprawled there taking some pleasure from the fresh air and an occasional piercing dart of sun, a dark suited man with a terribly deformed face came walking by. It was an unusual deformity, for though the skin was clean and unbroken, one could see that the right side of the face was involved in some gruesome disease which had swollen the jaw out of all proportion. The illness had perhaps destroyed the eye above the jaw, for the man wore dark glasses and under the right lens one could seen an eye patch, really more like a cup than a patch. The man's jaw worked constantly, quite apart it seemed from any volition of his own, as though it were ruminating on its own condition. But he went by, and as he did, I thought how in this city, the grotesque, both physical and mental, is frequently encountered.

Actually, it set my mind thinking of certain artists who often exploit physical disfiguration to indicate a kind of moral corruption. I was thinking in particular of a rather well-known film director who loved to make use of dwarves, of maimed and scale-eyed beggars in all sorts of tableaux. Such things can be effective in a soft and sentimental way. An audience, gripped by horror, will make an easy equation of physical and spiritual corruption, a fact which politicians and moralists have not ignored (indeed, one thinks of all those examples of the wages of sin inevitably depicted in terms of venereal disease or insanity).

Now wounds, it strikes me, may properly bear such a function, and yet how rare that is! For one may gaze somewhat ashamedly at the ambulatory veteran or the armless sleeve of a uniform at a parade and the spectre of social corruption will truly fly into one's brain—along with the image of bravery, etc.

But then, even these thoughts momentarily slipped from my mind as we entered the auditorium to see our friend dance. And sitting there in the darkness, I felt that very palpable thing, that pervasive eroticism of the taut beauty of the dancers in motion. Imagine my sudden shock then, after enjoying, after being absorbed in that severe grace, to have the house lights come on for the intermission and see, sitting only a few rows away, the man with the deformity, sopping away at his lips with a handkerchief, his jaw working furiously like a pestle in a mortar.

Curiously, I looked at the people on either side of him wondering how they responded to his presence. For where else but in great cities—now huge mill-ends and heaps of chaotic regularity —does the grotesque strike with such force, if we let it. In cities, where arrogantly we think (or thought) ourselves masters, the grotesque plays its hand with all the arbitrariness we thought conquered. Nevertheless, the people near the man were ignoring him.

See the contrast I suffered here: the impression of those superb bodies in the rigor of an art form, as against:

> the man's wish for a finely chiseled jaw
> of lips which could be controlled long enough
> to bestow a kiss,
> > dreams of impossibility
> that link to the thousands of dreams
> of being other than one was

How we were joined under the weight of this accidental insufficiency no more explicable than health and wholeness—that jaw ever-working, a *perpetuum mobile* of pain itself!

In that moment, all I could feel was contagion, a desire to leave.

But then my friend, who is often of amazingly good spirits, as though secretly reading my thoughts, pointed to the man and said, that must be the Critic. And he laughed and I laughed, but weakly, and only for my friend's humor. And when the performance ended, I hurried my wife and my friend out of the theater, making sure we took the aisle fathest from where the man had been sitting. And outside the air was fresh, *was fresh*, but the clouds tumbling across the immense panes of the building glass threw me again into a panic.

SUN

Address inquiries and catalogue requests to
SUN, 456 Riverside Drive, New York, NY 10027